Seventy-Seven
IRREFUTABLE TRUTHS OF PRAYER

Dr. Larry and Judi Keefauver

Bridge-Logos
Gainesville, Florida 32614 USA

The 77 Irrefutable Truths of Prayer
by Dr. Larry & Judi Keefauver

Copyright ©2003 by Bridge-Logos

All Rights Reserved
Printed in the United States of America
Library of Congress Catalog Card Number: Pending
ISBN: 0-8827-0909-7

Scripture taken from *THE MESSAGE*. Copyright ©1993,
1994, 1995, 1996, 2000, 2001, 2002. Used by permission of
NavPress Publishing Group.

Published by:
Bridge-Logos
P.O. Box 141630
Gainesville, FL 32614
www.bridgelogos.com

Editor: Dr. Larry Keefauver
Cover Design: Andy Toman
Interior Text Design/Layout: Cathleen Kwas

TABLE OF CONTENTS

PRAY *NOW*!

Prayer—it's over taught and underused. Reams of pages are written about it. Rivers of words flood through messages expounding it. But not enough praying happens.

Prayer's more than a noun; it's a verb.

Prayer acts.

Prayer speaks.

Prayer listens.

Prayer communes with God.

You're invited to implement these action-truths of prayer. Each "prayer act" releases God's promise of truth into life—yours and others.

Prayer *acts* by...

- speaking and listening
- crying and groaning
- asking and seeking.

This book was never intended to replace praying, only to prompt you to act *now!* As soon as you have read an action-truth, pray!

- Pray with the Spirit.
- Pray in agreement with a friend.
- Pray through your distractions and distracters.

- Pray out of your inner being, through your feelings and thoughts, to talk with the Lover of your soul.
- Pray for intimacy with the only One who is the answer to every question and need within you.
- Pray in the authority of the name of Jesus before whom every knee must bow in heaven and earth.

Father God, in the name of Jesus—full of authority and power, embolden your child to pray. With every obedient act of prayer, fill your child with the Spirit and truth to live in Christ. Amen.

So, friends, we can now—without hesitation— walk right up to God, into the "Holy Place." Jesus has cleared the way by the blood of his sacrifice, acting as our priest before God.
—Hebrews 10 (The Message)

1 PRAY TO START AND END YOUR DAY WITH GOD.

Evening and morning and at noon I will pray, and cry aloud, and He shall hear my voice.
— Psalm 55:7

Start with prayer. *It's called proactive prayer.* If you begin today with a negative, self-centered, problem-driven focus, then your day's spiritual forecast reads:

Cloudy

Storms Ahead

Lightning Alert

Prepare for a Shock!

Honestly, to begin the day talking to anyone except God gives you their perspective instead of His; their problems instead of His; and their direction instead of His. Focus your *day-starting* prayer on God not on things that you want or that distract you.

First-thought, first-talk, first-emotion prayer points you in the right direction and keeps you the head not the tail, the first and not the last, and the lender instead of the borrower (Deut. 28:12-13).

End with prayer. Your *day-ending* prayer isn't a mopping up action. It's thanks-giving, praise-proclaiming time celebrating all that God did with, through and in spite of you.

Starting your day without prayer guarantees a day ending

with tears, sorrow and distress. Starting your day with prayer ensures ending your day with eyes opened to new miracles, greater glory and incredible signs.

Think of it this way. Starting your day with prayer is like putting on glasses and seeing clearly both the visible and invisible. Without prayer, your day becomes like uncorrected vision so that you move ahead in a blurry, foggy haze not knowing when you'll stumble next.

Beginning prayer and ending prayer become the bookends for a day filled with dairies of divine communion.

> *God,*
> *I begin my day with You. Direct my steps. Unknot my emotions. Clear my head. Tune my Spirit to hear clearly the sounds of heaven. Amen.*

> *God,*
> *I end this day with You, thankful for your provision and protection, exulting in Your miracles, excited by Your leading, and rejoicing in Your forgiveness. Repenting of my sins, I ask You to refresh my spirit, rest my body, renew my mind, and restore my relationships. Amen.*

2 PRAY TO SOW TEARS FOR A BALM OF HEALING.

*Return and tell Hezekiah the leader of My people,
'Thus says the LORD, the God of David your
father: "I have heard your prayer, I have seen
your tears; surely I will heal you. On the third day
you shall go up to the house of the LORD." '"*
—2 Kings 20:5

Weeping prayer softens your heart to receive God's healing. When last did you weep for those lost whom you know? When last did you weep for anyone who is lost? When last did you weep for the sick in body, soul or spirit? When last did you weep for yourself?

Pray with tears.

Weeping prayer transforms the petitioner from a beggar into a penitent. Weeping never begs for something God does not will. God wills that all be saved. God wills that the sick be healed and the bound be delivered. God wills for the cleansing and purifying of one's soul.

Pray with tears for what God wills not what you want.

Let your heart be broken by what breaks God's heart. "Blessed are those who mourn, for they shall be comforted" (Matthew 5:4). Are you willing to weep for what God wills

5

instead of what you lack? We mourn our losses and grieve when we lack, but do we mourn for the lost and for what others lack?

Weeping prayer cleanses inner wounds
and primes the wellspring of healing.

Tears flow from a heart that breaks over all that breaks God's heart. Let the river of prayer flow to heal your inner wounds. Let the river of prayer wash away the dirt that clogs the well of living waters within you. Let the river of intercession flow from His throne through you and into the life of some who needs saving, healing or delivering.

God,
　　When you weep, give me Your tears,
Your tears for the poor and the rich,
Your tears for the sick and the healthy,
Your tears for the lonely and the crowded,
Your tears for the insiders and the outsiders,
Your tears for the grieving and the laughing,
Your tears for the weak and the powerful,
Your tears for the satisfied and unsatisfied,
Your tears for the depressed and the overjoyed,
Your tears for the oppressed and the oppressors,
For You have said that You will all to be saved.
　　So God let me pray for whomever You love, for whatever moves Your heart this moment, so that I will never neglect someone in prayer for whom Your heart breaks. Amen.

3 PRAY FOR GRACE TO UNLOCK GOD'S WAY TO DIVINE INTIMACY.

Now therefore, I pray, if I have found grace in Your sight, show me now Your way, that I may know You and that I may find grace in Your sight.
—Exodus 33:13

Grace can never be earned; it's always a gift. Prayer doesn't ask for grace; prayer accepts grace. Prayer says "Yes!" to grace.

Our problem in petitioning prayer stems from asking for what we want, instead of seeking what He desires to give. We make our lists and poll the lusts of our desires in order to present God with a gift list as if He is Santa Claus instead of the loving Father.

A loving Father always gives the grace that we need while wisely refusing to grant our wants. Receiving our wants puts us in bondage.

Like a child climbing into her Father's lap and laying her head upon his heart, draw close to your Father and he will draw close to you. Listen to His heart.

The Father's heart is generous, kind, loving and willing to bless us. We block God's grace through prayer by not trusting His heart. We believe that we know what's best for us and that God's only desire is to discipline and deprive us.

A contemporary song intunes, "When you can't see His hand, trust His heart." Intimacy means that we have drawn close to the Father's heart in prayer. Prayer, our spiritual stethoscope, listens to His heartbeat. The greatest gift of grace given through prayer is divine intimacy—the ability to hear the Father's heartbeat.

Stop begging or demanding. Pray for grace to draw near to His heart that you may hear what the Father has for you. Instead of demanding or begging begin listening and receiving. Listen to the Father's heart for what grace He has for you and then accept it.

What the Father has for you in prayer far exceeds anything you could beg for or demand. "Now to Him who is able to do exceedingly abundantly above all that we ask or think, according to the power that works in us to Him be glory in the church by Christ Jesus to all generations, forever and ever. Amen." (Eph. 3.20-21).

> *Jesus,*
> *I can't begin to imagine or ask You for what I really need today. Since You know the grace I need to receive, keep me close to Your heart that I may hear Your heart and know You intimately. Lord, right now I and say "Yes!" to Your grace. Amen.*

4 PRAY FOR YOUR CHILDREN.

For this child I prayed, and the LORD has granted me my petition which I asked of Him.
—1 Samuel 1:27

Pray for your children before their conception. Not just that conception will be ordinary but extraordinary. Hannah prayed for an extraordinary and miraculous conception. At the moment of conception, pray that God's hand fearfully and wonderfully forms a unique child filled with destiny.

Pray for your children in the womb. Not just that their births will go well but that their lives will prosper spiritually and naturally. Choose names of blessing so that whenever their names are spoken, blessing will be verbalized by you. Pray that God plants into their being His vision for their lives.

Pray for your children at birth. Not just for health but for well being. Pray for every dream that God has for them will be birthed within them. Pray that every vision God shows them will be clearly seen. Pray for their future mates and children so that your seed's seed will prosper.

Pray for your toddler. Not just that they will walk across the room but that they will walk through life with God. Not just that they will talk to you, but that they will talk with God.

Pray for your growing child. Not just that they will master words and math in school but that they will hide God's word in their hearts and learn God's math of tithing, giving and sowing.

Pray for your teenager. Not just that they (and you!) will survive the teen years, but that they will thrive, mature, and become godly adults. Pray not just for their graduation to be a completion but a commencement for greater accomplishments.

Pray for your adult child. Pray to bless their spouses. Pray that they will become as dear to you as your own flesh and blood. Pray that they will not only have work and money but will have others and money work for them so that they may build God's Kingdom. Pray that God would partner with you for the good inheritance you will leave your children and children's children. "A good man leaves an inheritance to his children's children" (Prov. 13:22).

Oh God,

Grant me the wisdom to amass a lasting, good inheritance for my children and children's children. Empower me my Your Spirit to pray into their lives the blessing of Your Presence while breaking every curse of the past through the precious, shed blood of Jesus. In conception, be Thou their inception. In the womb, be Thou their name. In birth, be Thou their vision. In childhood, be Thou their teacher. In the teen years, be Thou their counsel. In the adult years, be Thou their wisdom.

Oh God,

Into my children I sow the seed of Your Word, the anointing of Your Spirit, and the love of Your Father heart. Amen.

5 PRAY TO LIFT YOUR FAINTING SOUL INTO GOD'S PRESENCE.

When my soul fainted within me, I remembered the LORD; and my prayer went up to You, into Your holy temple.

—Jonah 2:7

What weakens the soul? *Problems, pressure, perplexity, persecution* and *plagues* all position your soul on the precipice of fainting.

Prayer transforms *problems* into possibilities. When problems erode away the soul's strength, focus in prayer on God's possibilities. We are tempted to fix our eyes on the problems instead of the person of Christ who unravels every twisted, tortured thought within our souls. "With men it is impossible, but not with God; for with God all things are possible" (Mark 10:27).

Prayer pushes *pressure* aside. Pressure or stress can only crush you if let it accumulate. Push pressure into the past. Refuse to carry yesterday's stress and worries into the present. Don't allow tomorrow's worries to intrude into today's agenda. "But we have this treasure in earthen vessels, that the excellence of the power may be of God and not of us. We are hard pressed on every side, yet not crushed" (2 Cor. 4:7-8).

Prayer clarifies *perplexity*. The enemy authors confusion. Pray that God's clarity will cleanse the windows of your mind giving you unclouded vision for your next step. "We are perplexed but not in despair" (2 Cor. 4:8).

Prayer transforms *persecution* into blessing. "*We are* persecuted, but not forsaken" (2 Cor. 4:9). Jesus declares in Matthew 5 that we are blessed when others persecute us. Prayer projects on the screen of our hearts the picture of Jesus on the cross so that we can suffer with Him and thereby rejoice with Him. "That I may know Him and the power of His resurrection, and the fellowship of His sufferings, being conformed to His death" (Phil. 3:10).

Prayer positions my *plagued* soul next to the Healer of every soul. When I am sick unto despair or sick in body, what I need more than a healing is the Healer. The Lover of my soul takes whatever sin makes me faint and nails that sin to the cross. "By His stripes we are healed" (Isa. 53:5). In prayer I come to the Healer. In His presence, I find that my soul is restored and my body is made whole. Pray this:

Bless the LORD, O my soul,
And forget not all His benefits:
Who forgives all your iniquities,
Who heals all your diseases,
Who redeems your life from destruction,
Who crowns you with lovingkindness and tender
  mercies,
Who satisfies your mouth with good things,
So that your youth is renewed like the eagle's.
Amen.

(from Psalm 103:2-5)

6 PRAY THE JESUS WAY.

In this manner, therefore, pray: our Father in heaven, hallowed be Your name.

–Matthew 6:9

Jesus taught us the way of prayer. The prayer He gave to his disciples models for us the basic elements of our every conversation with the Father.

Larry Lea pointed to each of these elements as starting with "P." I have adapted these as follows:

Papa. Jesus calls God, "Abba." He is our Father, our Papa, who loves and cares for us. *Our Father in heaven.*

Proclamation. We cry "Holy" with the angels in praise and honor to glorify God the King. His name is holy. To all flesh, we proclaim the name of the Lord. *Hallowed be Your name.*

Providence. As King, God has established His providence over all creation. Through habitual grace, God sustains His Kingdom as the rain falls on the just and the unjust. *Your kingdom come, Your will be done on earth as it is in heaven.*

Provision. God takes care of us. He alone is our source. Not our jobs, our spouse, our saving or our strength can be our source. God alone provides. *Give us this day our daily bread.*

Pardon. God alone forgives sin. Through the shed blood of Jesus, God cleanses us from iniquity. Confessing our sins, He is faithful and just to forgive us (1 John 1:9). Receiving forgiveness arises not from our merit but from our willingness to forgive. Unforgiveness hardens our hearts to receiving His forgiveness. *Forgive us our debts, as we forgive our debtors.*

Protection. No weapon formed against us will prosper. Attacks may come from every side but God is our sure defense and strong tower. Under the shadow of His outstretched wings we abide and find refuge (Psalm 91). *And lead us not into temptation, but deliver us from the evil one.*

Power and Praise. No power can annul the purposes of God. No device of the enemy can thwart His good plans to prosper us. God inhabits our praise and conquers every foe. *For yours is the kingdom, and the power, and the glory forever. Amen.*

Our Father in heaven, Hallowed be Your name.
Your kingdom come. Your will be done
On earth as it is in heaven.
Give us this day our daily bread.
And forgive us our debts,
As we forgive our debtors.
And do not lead us into temptation,
But deliver us from the evil one.
For Yours is the kingdom and the power
and the glory forever. Amen.

7 PRAY TO HURT NO ONE.

And Jabez called on the God of Israel saying, "Oh, that You would bless me indeed, and enlarge my territory, that Your hand would be with me, and that You would keep me from evil, that I may not cause pain!" So God granted him what he requested.

—1 Chron. 4:10

Our blessing never comes as an expense to others. God doesn't steal from others to give to us. Our prosperity does not rob others of what they need. God gives to us out of His abundance not from other's poverty.

But out of our abundance we may cause pain. We may use what we have to curse rather than bless others. Instead of being blessed to be a blessing, we can choose to hoard, hurt and harm others with our wealth.

Pray that whatever you profess or possess will not pain others. Paul interceded for the Corinthians, "I pray to God that you do no evil" (2 Cor. 13:7).

Pray that your blessing never becomes your bane. Ask God to grant you a full pound of humility with every ounce of prosperity.

Pray to give that you might receive instead of praying to get that you might give. Givers are in constant need of more to give while "getters" are in constant need of ways to store what they hoard. The rich man built barns to store his possessions and met an early demise (Luke 12). The widow gave all she had and garnered the praise of the Savior (Mark 12).

Should you discover that you have hurt another, causing pain, or creating lack in their lives, pray for a willingness to restore sevenfold (Prov. 6:30-31).

Lord,

Shape my life into a vessel of pouring... pouring out blessing, pouring out kindness and gentleness, pouring out praise, pouring out love, pouring out healing and hope.

May I never cause others pain or hurt. but if I should, bring me to quick repentance and a generous willingness to restore sevenfold. Amen.

8 PRAY WITH VIGILANCE.

Continue earnestly in prayer, being vigilant in it with thanksgiving.

–Colossians 4:2

The vigilant keep watch. Become a watchman on the tower with your prayers. God said to Ezekiel, "I have made you a watchman" (Ezek. 3:17).

Watch for the enemy. As the watchman stands guard on the wall, he spies the enemy coming from afar. Sounding the alarm, the watchman alerts the city to a coming attack. Remember to pray for the Lord to guard the city or you will watch vainly in prayer (Ps. 127:1). Be watchful in prayer lest the devil seek you out and devour you (1 Peter 5:8).

Watch for the coming of the Lord. The watchman sees the sword of the Lord approaching (Ezek. 33). He proclaims the coming of the Day of the Lord. Ever vigilant and ready, the watchman in prayer knows the voice of the Lord and the sound of His approach.

Vigilant prayer prophesies.

Vigilant prayer is the prayer of the seer. "For thus has the Lord said to me: 'Go, set a watchman, Let him declare what he sees'" (Isa. 21:6).

Vigilant prayer births that which is seen prophetically.
Elijah assumed a position of birthing and saw by the prayer of
faith the rain that was coming.

> *And Elijah went up to the top of Carmel; then he
> bowed down on the ground, and put his face
> between his knees, and said to his servant, "Go
> up now, look toward the sea." So he went up and
> looked, and said, "There is nothing." And seven
> times he said, "Go again." Then it came to pass
> the seventh time, that he said, "There is a cloud,
> as small as a man's hand, rising out of the sea!"*
> —1 Kings 18:42-44

**Vigilant prayer never gives up, never quits, and never
abandons the post.** As long as the watch requires, the
watchman alertly prays. Slumber tempts but cannot prevail.
Fatigue weakens but cannot overcome. Impatience threatens
but cannot erode the patient assurance and confident hope that
steels the watchman in vigilant prayer.

> *Almighty God,*
> *Keep me awake in prayer. Let sleeplessness be
> my spiritual state. As I pray, permit me to see the
> coming attacks, that I may alert my household,
> and prepare to stand firm. As I watch with
> vigilance, reveal to me when your coming rain,
> that I might prophesy your refreshing. Amen.*

9 PRAY TO SHAKE THE PLACE.

And when they had prayed, the place where they were assembled together was shaken; and they were all filled with the Holy Spirit, and they spoke the word of God with boldness.

—Acts 4:31

Prayer shakes the place where we assemble. We cannot expect to be the church as usual when we pray. We can expect change. Instead of praying, "God change others," we must begin praying, "God change me."

We are salt in the world. As we pray, God shakes the saltshaker and out we are thrust into the world for which we have prayed. Praying has no power without going. Going has no mission without praying.

Prayer shakes the person praying. The place of prayer is never a building; it's always a person. We are the temples of the Holy Spirit. We are the dwelling place of the living God. God shakes everything through prayer so that what cannot be shaken will remain (Heb. 12:27-28).

Prayer shakes the world prayed for. When we pray, the world is turned upside down (Acts 17:6). Prayer that shakes us, sends us into a world that needs to hear a bold proclamation of the gospel.

Too often praying people are viewed as wimps instead of warriors. Too often praying people are hidden away in a back room instead of boldly declaring what God has said on the street corner.

Shaken people in prayer have nothing to fear, nothing to hide and nothing to lose in following Christ out of the closet and into the world. Having been shaken by God, warriors in prayer cannot be shaken by anything in the world.

> *Lord,*
> *Shake me. Rattle me. Disturb me. Discomfort and disquiet me. Shake out of me anything that is not tied to You. Loosen from me anything that binds me up. Shake me free from all bondages so that I will boldly proclaim You to all who are lost. Amen.*

10 KEEP PRAYING TO AVOID SINNING AGAINST THE LORD.

Moreover, as for me, far be it from me that I should sin against the LORD in ceasing to pray for you; but I will teach you the good and the right way.

—1 Samuel 12:23

Prayerlessness sins against God and others. God's will moves from eternity into time through prayer.

God has intended for His bride, the church, to pray "thy will be done on earth as it is in heaven." When we fail to pray, the invisible does not become visible and the substance for which we believe remains still hoped for.

Prayerlessness is sin; it separates us from God.

Without prayer, communion ceases.

Without prayer, nothing happens, as E.M. Bounds wisely instructed.

Without prayer, the Spirit remains uninvited to move through us by His gifts and produce in us His fruit.

With prayer, sin is confessed and cleansed away.

With prayer, communication with God becomes a river of living water and a consuming fire burning away our dross and refining our faith.

With prayer, our ears are opened to hear the incredible.

With prayer, our eyes are opened to see the invisible.

With prayer, our lives are empowered to do the impossible.

Therefore, prayerlessness breeds more than neglect in our lives. It offers up the stench of sin and the putrid odor of wasted and unfilled dreams.

Prayer becomes the sweet odor of a living sacrifice offered up to God as you worship Him on the altar of obedience. Build the altar of prayer now. Let your sin be consumed by the fire of His Spirit. Let your life become a sweet aroma as the smell of being with Him permeates your talk and your walk.

I come to You, Lord Jesus, in obedience, offering myself to You as a living sacrifice, that I may worship and serve You. As I pray, consume me with the fire of Your Spirit, that the odor of my life might be sweet to You and the scent of Your presence as a testimony for the lives of others. Amen.

·

11 PRAY TO RELEASE RESURRECTION POWER.

And he stretched himself out on the child three times, and cried out to the LORD and said, "O LORD my God, I pray, let this child's soul come back to him."

—1 Kings 17:21

Prayer is the conduit through which God's life flows from heaven to earth. Prayer digs a new well tapping into a fresh spring of living water that flows from the river of God's Spirit.

When last did you pray for life to enter into a dead man's body? The lost are dead. Are you praying for the lost?

The proud are dead. Are you praying for death to self and life in Christ?

The living dead move about us crying out for life. Theirs is merely existence.

Existence pictures reality in black and white instead of color. Existence sounds like a monotone instead of stereo. Existence knows only lack and never abundance. Existence crawls through the wilderness of loneliness without ever experiencing lasting friendship. Existence tastes like stale bread and water. Existence stumbles on every curse and bypasses every blessing. Existence only prays one prayer, "Help!"

Life comes from its creator—God. In His presence, we live, move and have our being. Prayer breathes life—life into us and through us.

Life eats fresh bread and drinks fresh water through prayer. Prayer is the tether in life that keeps us connected to God.

Cover that which is dead in prayer. Let resurrection power flow through you into what just exists. Just existing never satisfies. Living brings wholeness and fulfillment. Prayer breathes life into existence.

Prayer listens to the Father's words and then speaks them to others. As Jesus said, "I do nothing of Myself; but as My Father taught Me, I speak these things" (John 8:28-29). Prayer imparts the life of God in me into others.

> *Father,*
> *Speak words of life to me that I may speak life to others.*
>
> *Jesus,*
> *Incarnate your words of life in me that I may be life to others.*
>
> *Spirit,*
> *Breathe prophetic words of life through me that I may prophesy life to others. Amen.*

12 PRAY BEFORE THE BATTLE.

When Your people go out to battle against their enemy, wherever You send them, and when they pray to the LORD toward the city which You have chosen and the temple which I have built for Your name, then hear in heaven their prayer and their supplication, and maintain their cause.

—1 Kings 8:44-45

Before Israel went into battle, Solomon prayed entreating God for victory.

Before battling Jericho, the people of Israel marched, blew the trumpets and then shouted to the Lord. Before the battle of Jericho, God revealed to Joshua that the city was already his— the battle was already won! (Read Joshua 6:1-2)

Before battling the Midianites, Gideon spoke with the Lord, built an altar of worship, and obeyed what God told him.

Before battling Goliath, David declared that the battle belonged to the Lord.

Before facing the Assyrians in battle, King Hezekiah prayed unto the Lord and the battle was won by God before any stone was cast or weapon thrown.

Before facing the Ammonites and Moabites in battle, King Jehoshaphat and the people bowed before God, praised Him and stood still to see the salvation of the Lord (2 Chron. 20).

Before facing the battle of Golgotha and triumphing over the enemies of death and sin on the cross, Jesus prayed in Gethsemane, "Thy will not mine be done."

Here's the prayer key we need to understand: *proactive prayer anticipates both the coming battle and the victory that God has already won.*

Be proactive not reactive. Our tendency in prayer is to be reactive instead of proactive. In the midst of the battle when the tide turns against us, then we cry out, "Oh God, save me." Our problem is that we have entered the battle in our own strength and fought with our own weapons instead of fighting the battle God's way with His weapons. "For the weapons of our warfare are not carnal but mighty in God for pulling down strongholds" (2 Cor. 10:4).

Pray before the battle. Get the mind of the Lord for the battle. Ask God to maintain His cause and purpose for the battle. Rest in the truth that the battle is never against flesh and blood (Eph. 6). Remember that the enemy is never the other person but always the father of lies who seek to steal, kill and destroy (John 10:10).

> *Spirit of God,*
> *Capture my attention before any battle. Keep my focus on you not the enemy. Reveal to me the device and wiles of the enemy. Release your power and might to win the victory. I praise you in advance for the victory! Amen.*

13 BRING AN OFFERING WITH YOUR PRAYER.

Do not depart from here, I pray, until I come to You and bring out my offering and set it before You.

—Judges 6:18

Gideon prayed and brought an offering to God. Giving and praying go hand in hand as we walk in the Spirit.

The Hebrews worshipped, prayed and brought their offerings to the Lord. We read how David brought offerings and prayers before God to rebuke a plague from God's people.

"And David built there an altar to the LORD, and offered burnt offerings and peace offerings. So the LORD heeded the prayers for the land, and the plague was withdrawn from Israel" (2 Sam. 24:25).

In the New Testament, they prayed and sold their goods to bring offerings for the needs of God's people (Acts 2:42-47). Cornelius gave alms to the poor and prayed. This resulted in the salvation of his household (Acts 10).

Pray and give. Give and pray. The synergy of prayer and giving builds a lasting memorial before God.

God,
To you I bring the offerings of my treasure, time and talents. I pray that you will accept my prayers and offerings as a memorial before your face. Amen.

14 PRAY FOR POWER.

And now, I pray, let the power of my LORD be great, just as You have spoken."
—Numbers 14:17

Confess. Praying for power begins with a confession.

Lord, I can't but You can.

It's not by personal might or power but by His Spirit that anything is accomplished in our lives (Zech. 4:6).

Repent. Praying for power involves repentance.

I repent of trying instead of trusting You, Lord.

Repent of trying to do it yourself. Repent of using power for your own purposes and promotion. Repent of depending on anything or anyone other than God.

Praise. Praying for power gives God the praise and the glory.

I praise you, Lord, for what You have done and will do through me.

Proclaim. Proclaim the name of the Lord over everyone and everything around you.

In Jesus' name is all power and authority. Amen.

15 PRAY FOR PARDON AS AN ADOPTED HEIR.

If now I have found grace in Your sight, O Lord, let my Lord, I pray, go among us, even though we are a stiff-necked people; and pardon our iniquity and our sin, and take us as Your inheritance.

—Exodus 34:9

We have been adopted (Romans 8). Our adoption as the heirs of God gives us the privilege of claiming our inheritance in prayer.

When we present a withdrawal slip or write a check on our account in the bank, we expect to have funds available to us. On our behalf, God has made a deposit for us, his heirs, in the name of Christ Jesus in heaven.

We draw upon our inheritance of life, power, authority, and abundance as we pray. The pin number that accesses our account is JESUS. That access code has been given to us through His pardon of our sins.

In prayer, claim your inheritance. The pardon has been granted. The deposit has been made. In the deposit of His Spirit we have received all that we need to operate as His heirs.

"In Him you also trusted, after you heard the word of truth, the gospel of your salvation; in whom also, having believed, you were sealed with the Holy Spirit of promise, who is the guarantee of our inheritance until the redemption of the purchased possession, to the praise of His glory" (Eph. 1:13-14).

Father,

As Your adopted child through the blood of Jesus, I claim my inheritance of life, abundance, power, grace, favor, and glory, so that I may live in power and authority, to do and declare Your will in every area of my life. Amen.

16 ASK IN PRAYER TO RECEIVE.

You lust and do not have. You murder and covet and cannot obtain. You fight and war. Yet you do not have because you do not ask.

—James 4:2

What keeps us from asking for what we truly need?

- **Pride**. We are too proud to ask.

- **Ignorance**. We don't know how to ask or what to ask for.

- **Lust**. We ask for the wrong thing lusting for what we want instead of what we need.

- **Doubt**. We don't have the faith or trust in God that He will really move on our behalf.

- **Anger**. We are angry with God or someone else and that anger walls us out from receiving what God wants us to have.

- **Greed**. We want for ourselves instead of for the kingdom.

- **Hurt**. We allow our pain to block our healing.

- **Relief**. We want relief more than correction, discipline or restoration.

So what's really keeping you from asking? Whatever it is, repent. Let God change your heart so that you can pray for what He wants instead of your own selfish desires.

Oh God,

Teach me what I need and how to ask so that I will receive from You what is needful in Your kingdom. Amen.

17 PRAY FOR MORE THAN HELP; PRAY FOR THE HELPER.

And I will pray the Father, and He will give you another Helper, that He may abide with you forever.

—John 14:16

What is the most universal prayer prayed? *Lord, help!* When is the most common time that people pray? *Anytime they need **help!***

Jesus has great news for you. You can stop waiting until you need help to pray for it. In fact, you'll never have to pray "Help!" again. Why? Because *the Helper,* also known as the "Comforter" or the "Counselor" is available to anticipate your needs and help you even before you know you're going to need help!

Jesus has breathed the Holy Spirit into us for one purpose...to help. He helps us pray when we don't know how to pray (Romans 8).

The Spirit helps us make wise decisions so we won't always be crying "Help!" after making foolish decisions. The indwelling Holy Spirit imparts knowledge, wisdom, understanding and power to us (Isa. 11:2). That means we not only can know what's right; we have the power to do what's right!

So what are you waiting for? If you are not a follower of Jesus, repent of your past sins, be baptized and receive the gift of the Holy Spirit (Acts 2:38). If you are a follower of Jesus, stop crying out for help. Instead, cry out for the Helper to always guide and direct your ways.

Jesus,
I receive the Holy Spirit, the Helper into my life.
Amen.

18 ABIDE PATIENTLY IN PRAYER.

Continuing steadfastly in prayer.

—Romans 12:12

This phrase in the Greek implies that we need to dwell, abide, even to rest in prayer. Urgent prayer isn't about needing an answer *now*. Praying with urgency has to do with being urgent to get alone with God, to withdraw immediately into His presence, to rush to meet with Him *now*.

Once there, once we enter the secret place under the shadow of His wings (Ps. 91), we can rest, abide, wait patiently and confidently in Him. Before we prayed, His answer was there. Before we came, He was waiting for us. Before we asked, He had prepared a table, yes even a feast for us.

Jesus stands at the door of our hearts (Rev. 3:20) and knocks. We are the ones resisting not God. We are the ones restless, not God.

Abiding patiently in prayer means…

- Always keeping our heart's door open to Jesus.
- Always trusting that His way and timing are best..
- Always resting in Him instead of rushing around trying to find Him.
- Always dwelling at His place instead of maintaining our place.

- Always waiting for Him instead of impatiently wanting from Him.
- Always listening without interrupting.

Prayer isn't talking with God on our terms; prayer listens to God abiding by His terms. When we feel God hasn't answered, it's only a feeling. Feelings are always real but not always reality.

The truth is that God always answers but we must patiently wait for His timing and way. I want an answer in my time. He gives His answer in His time.

Abiding patiently in prayer is hard until we finally surrender our will to His, our way to His and our wants to His.

God,
Grant me the patience to wait for Your answer, instead of lobbying incessantly for my answer. Grant me the desire to unlock the door and throw away the key, so that You always have free access to my soul. Amen.

19 SANCTIFY IT BY PRAYER.

For it is sanctified by the word of God and prayer.
—1 Timothy 4:5

Sanctify. Make holy. Separate. Consecrate. Dedicate. Set apart to be used exclusively by God.

It. What's "it?" *It* is anything and everything. *It* is anyone and everyone.

It is anything you are about to do or say. Before you do *it*, make certain in prayer that the Father has told you to do *it*. Before you say *it*, be sure by prayer that the Father has told you to say *it*.

It is everything you thing, feel or will. *It* is everything you plan, wish for or dream about. Some people refuse to go outside before checking out the weather on the TV or radio. Some people refuse to invest any of their money until they have checked with their broker. Some athletes and authors will not sign a deal until they have talked with their agent or attorney.

What about you? Who sets things apart in your life? Who gives approval before you take the next step? True surrender means that everything in life is sanctified by prayer. No trip, no purchase, no decision, no word or action is taken without first sanctifying it by prayer. E.M. Bounds asserted that nothing happens without prayer.

By prayer, the believer hears from God first and then communicates with others.

By prayer, the believer sanctifies or dedicates everything to God's use. A.W. Tozer counseled us to "own nothing." If everything including possessions has been consecrated to God by prayer, then we have surrendered all rights and become stewards instead of owners. A steward knows that everything in his hand including his own life belongs to another.

Once "it" is sanctified by prayer, you can no longer pick *it* up, claim *it*, use *it*, or neglect *it* according to your own volition. *It* belongs to God.

> *Lord Jesus,*
> *I dedicate everything by prayer to You. All that I am and do is dedicated to You. Be glorified in my life. Show me the glory of sanctifying all to You. Amen.*

20 PRAY RIGHTEOUSLY TO BE SEEN AND HEARD BY GOD.

For the eyes of the LORD are on the righteous,
And His ears are open to their prayers.

—1 Peter 3:12

Interesting isn't it? He who never slumbers or sleeps is always attentive to our prayers. God always listens, but does He always take notice of what we say? Yes, God sees everything, but does He really look at what we want Him to see?

Here's the key to effective prayer: *righteousness.* Righteousness is right position. Think of it this way. Dial a wrong number; get the wrong party. Use the wrong pin number; get no money at the ATM. Write the wrong email; get no answer back.

How does one come into a right position or relationship with God so that our prayers are seen and heard by Him, i.e. our prayers are effective in partnering with God to have his will in heaven done on earth in our lives?

THE ABC'S OF ANSWERED PRAYER

Abide. *Abide in Christ.* (Read John 15.) Christ is our righteousness (1 Cor. 1:30). In Christ we are empowered to walk in the Spirit (Rom. 8:1). Walking in the Spirit we have fellowship with Him which leads to that abiding that results in answered prayer. "If you abide in Me, and My words abide in you, you will ask what you desire, and it shall be done for you" (Jn. 15:7).

Believe. *Have faith in God not prayer.* Prayer doesn't make things happen, God does. Abraham's faith counted for righteousness (Gen. 15:16). Jesus tells us to trust without reservation, "I tell you the truth, if anyone says to this mountain, 'Go, throw yourself into the sea,' and does not doubt in his heart but believes that what he says will happen, it will be done for him" (Mark 11:23-24 NIV).

Continue. *"Pray continually"* (1 Thess. 5:17 NIV). Continually persevere in prayer. Don't give up. Stay close to God and continue to talk and listen, petition and intercede (Luke 18:1-8; 2 Peter 1:5-8).

Remember the parable of the persistent widow who cried out for justice from an evil judge? Jesus reminds us, "If even an evil judge can be worn down like that, don't you think that God will surely give justice to his people who plead with him day and night?" (Luke 18:6-17).

Sometimes I am put on hold when talking on the phone. If I get tired of waiting, I may break the connection and hang up. In doing so, I never finish the conversation. The same is true of prayer. If we quit praying, the answers will stop flowing.

Lord,
Pull me away from attachments that with You
I may abide. Impart within me a great intensity of
faith. Grant me the resilience to continue. Amen.

21 COME BOLDLY IN PRAYER.

Let us therefore come boldly to the throne of grace, that we may obtain mercy and find grace to help in time of need.

—Hebrews 4:16

Boldly isn't arrogantly for our approach has nothing to do with our own merit (Eph. 2:8).

Boldly isn't proudly for our coming isn't of our own effort but through the shed blood of Jesus the Christ (Heb. 9).

Boldly is shamelessly. Christ hath borne our shame and washed away our sins (Isa. 53, 1 John 1).

Boldly is freely. We come without duty but in thanksgiving with a sacrifice of praise (Heb. 13:15).

Boldly is confidently. We have every confidence in the efficacy of Christ to accomplish more than we can every think or imagine (Eph. 3:20, Heb. 6:9).

Therefore, stop begging, cowering, sniveling, whining, stuttering, and crawling. Start praising, proclaiming, worshipping, celebrating and dancing in joy for what the Lord will accomplish through your coming in prayer into His presence.

22 PRAY CONFIDENTLY.

Now this is the confidence that we have in Him, that if we ask anything according to His will, He hears us. And if we know that He hears us, whatever we ask, we know that we have the petitions that we have asked of Him.

—1 John 5:14

Confidence in prayer rests not in what or how I pray but in whom I pray. Some believe prayer is a formula that manipulates God into acting because they have said all the right things in the right way. Formula prayer is magic not communion with the living God. Confident prayer know with certainty that:

God always listens. We can't miss God in prayer. He's always there. Jesus promises to be with us always (Mt. 28). God promises never to leave or forsake us (Heb. 12). Therefore we cannot miss our omnipresent and loving God. He's never on voicemail or vacation. He's always ready for dialogue. "Come now, and let us reason together" (Isa. 1:18).

God always answers. That answer comes according to His providence and sovereignty. God's timing will put us into a process that fulfills His will for His glory. Are you willing to accept His answer?

God,
Open my ears to Your answers; raise my faith to me
Your provision; open my heart to Your direction. Amen.

23 PRAY FOR WHAT'S LASTING.

Let my prayer be set before You as incense.
—Psalm 141:2

The prayers of the saints rise eternally as a sweet aroma of incense before the throne of God. "Now when He had taken the scroll, the four living creatures and the twenty-four elders fell down before the Lamb, each having a harp, and golden bowls full of incense, which are the prayers of the saints" (Rev. 5:8-8).

Saints pray for what's lasting, what's invisible, what's eternal and what's close to the heart of God. Stop whining and complaining to God. Stop asking God for stuff outside of His will. Stop seeking for what's of the flesh and not of the Spirit.

Too many Christians put up a stink before His throne instead of offering to God the sweet aroma of the sacrifice of praise and thanksgiving.

Stinking thinking leads to stinking praying. Stinking praying defiles us and never lasts before the throne of God; it evaporates into the winds of time.

Praying for what lasts is praying God's kingdom to earth. Pray for workers in the harvest. Pray for souls to be saved.

Pray for God's Spirit to empower you to do good works in serving "the least of these" and "giving a cup of water in Jesus' name."

Jesus,

    Save my family, friends and enemies. Grant me the resources to serve the poor. Make my life and prayers count for eternity. Amen.

24 PRAY TO OPEN EYES.

And Elisha prayed, and said, "LORD, I pray, open his eyes that he may see." Then the LORD opened the eyes of the young man, and he saw. And behold, the mountain was full of horses and chariots of fire all around Elisha.

—2 Kings 6:17

Prayer opens our eyes to see the invisible. *Thy kingdom come, thy will be done, on earth as it is in heaven* is an invitation to God's Spirit to open our eyes to see what God wants to do in, through and around us.

Pray for God to open your eyes and the eyes of others to the miracles, signs and wonders He works continually. People don't see miracles not because He isn't at work but because they are blinded to His work.

Pray for God to open your eyes and the eyes of others to sin. Pride blinds us to sin. Surrender and repentance opens us to see those things in us that separate us from God and others.

Pray for God to open your eyes and the eyes of others to pain. When we see pain, we will know how to pray for comfort and healing.

Pray for God to open your eyes and the eyes of others to lack. When we see the lack, we will know how to pray for provision and blessing.

Pray for God to open your eyes and the eyes of others to

curses. When we see the curses and strongholds, we will know how to pray for breaking every curse and shattering every stronghold.

Pray for God to open your eyes and the eyes of others to rebellion. In seeing rebellion, we will know how to pray for humility, submission and surrender. And we will understand how to submit to godly authority.

> *Almighty God,*
> *Open my eyes to see all that You are doing and all that You are exposing so that I may see myself and others as You see them. Amen.*

25 PRAY FOR RIGHT TIMING.

But as for me, my prayer is to You, O LORD, in the acceptable time;

—Psalm 69:13

Too often I pray for *my timing* instead of *His timing.* I want what I want now! I push to see my timeline or timetable accomplished so that I will be comforted and satisfied.

However, the *acceptable time* always comes when God's way and will are implemented for His glory. God's perfect timing brings people, resources and circumstances into the alignment He has ordered and ordained.

In an acceptable time, God answers our prayers to accomplish His purposes not ours. God says, "In an acceptable time I have heard You, And in the day of salvation I have helped You; I will preserve You and give You As a covenant to the people, To restore the earth, To cause them to inherit the desolate heritages" (Isa. 49:8). God's acceptable time demonstrates His faithfulness to others through us.

God's acceptable time brings forth salvation, i.e. eternal relationship with God, healing and deliverance. Don't push for another time in prayer; petition for God's acceptable time.

O Lord,
Execute your will in your acceptable time in every aspect of my life. Amen.

26 PRAY WITH FASTING TO SEE DELIVERANCE.

However, this kind does not go out except by prayer and fasting.

—Matthew 17:21

Prayer applies God's power and healing to the situation. Fasting applies our attention and focus.

Pray centers our mind on God. Fasting takes our mind off of our needs and fixes our minds on His needs.

Prayer surrenders wants. Fasting lets go of wants and cries out for what God desires.

Prayer seeks, knocks and asks. Fasting receives, opens and answers. In fasting, I deny myself physical food in order to receive spiritual food, i.e. the bread of life. In fasting, I unlock the inner chambers of my heart to open myself to all the light and revelation God wants me to have. In fasting, I cease asking God questions and I begin answering God's inquiries of me.

In prayer, I connect with God. Prayer is like plugging in a power cord. Fasting, like turning on the switch, releases the power to change me and those around me.

Prayer takes me up from earth to heaven; fasting brings heaven to earth. Fasting empties me of earth so that heaven might fill me.

Prayer vacates my soul of self so that fasting can produce such hunger and thirst for God that nothing but God can satisfy.

Prayer digs the well. Fasting keeps the well cleaned out.

Lord,

Give me a willingness to pray and fast, a humility to receive what that will bring, and obedience to do whatever it takes to follow Your Spirit. Amen.

27 PRAY TO RECEIVE THE HOLY SPIRIT.

*When they had come down, [he] prayed for them
that they might receive the Holy Spirit.*

—Acts 8:15

How welcome is the Holy Spirit in your life? Oh, you may have asked Him to fill, baptize, anoint, counsel and comfort you. But have you really meant it? Did you sincerely welcome the Spirit into your life?

To receive the Holy Spirit demands of us a willingness to receive all He has for us—transformation, change, power, gifts, and fruit.

Receiving the Holy Spirit means that your life will constantly change. That's uncomfortable. That's unplanned and unpredictable. Are you willing to receive how the Spirit will change and transform you?

Receiving the Holy Spirit means that you have relinquished power over your life Him. Now, every thought, feeling and decision is subject to His authority. Are you willing to receive the Spirit's power?

Receiving the Holy Spirit means that you are willing to be used by Him. And it means you are willing to bear fruit in your life for him.

Jesus,
I pray to receive Your Spirit. Amen.

28 FAST AND PRAY BEFORE LAYING ON HANDS.

Then, having fasted and prayed, and laid hands on them, they sent them away.

—Acts 13:3

Laying on hands imparts and conveys the Spirit and blessing of God. Don't lay hands on others lightly and without first asking the Spirit what you are to pray and say.

Laying on hands ordains and commissions. Without knowing the Spirit's direction, you cannot know where to send or what mission is being commissioned.

Laying on hands heals and restores. What is it that the Spirit wishes to heal? What's obvious to one's senses or reason may not be what the Spirit desires to touch and make whole.

So fast before laying on hands.

Fast to receive spiritual food. Fast to set aside the flesh's desires. Flesh to avoid manipulating, intimidating or dominating the one receiving the laying on of hands.

So pray before laying on hands.

Pray to have the mind of Christ. Pray to stir up and emblazen the gifts within you. Pray to become a vessel used of the Spirit. Pray to hear the Spirit's voice. Pray to release whatever the Spirit desires.

Fast and fast before laying on hands so that you may only be the conduit through whom the Spirit's power and anointing flows.

Spirit of the living God,

I pray that You would lead me to lay hands on the sick that they may recover, on the bound that they may be loosed, on the blind that they may see. Amen.

29 REJOICE WHEN YOU PRAY.

Always in every prayer of mine making request for you all with joy.

—Philippians 1:4

Laugh. Celebrate. Praise. Overflow with joy when you pray. Why are you so somber? Perhaps you take yourself too seriously when you pray!

There is a time to weep and a time to laugh declares the preacher in Ecclesiastes 3:4. So why do you spend so much time anguishing in prayer. Laugh!

Jesus rejoiced when he prayed:

> *In that hour Jesus rejoiced in the Spirit and said, "I thank You, Father, Lord of heaven and earth, that You have hidden these things from the wise and prudent and revealed them to babes. Even so, Father, for so it seemed good in Your sight."*
>
> (Luke 10:21-22).

Why rejoice? Rejoice because He will answer your prayer. Rejoice because the victory of the Cross has already been won. Rejoice because you have received the gift of the Holy Spirit. Rejoice because abundant life is yours. Rejoice because you cannot fail. Rejoice because the best is yet to come.

Let Psalm 150 be the climate in which your prayers rise to the Father, i.e. praise the Lord in everything!

Praise the LORD!
Praise God in His sanctuary;
Praise Him in His mighty firmament!
Praise Him for His mighty acts;
Praise Him according to His excellent greatness!
Praise Him with the sound of the trumpet;
Praise Him with the lute and harp!
Praise Him with the timbrel and dance;
Praise Him with stringed instruments and flutes!
Praise Him with loud cymbals;
Praise Him with clashing cymbals!
Let everything that has breath praise the LORD.
Praise the LORD!

          —Psalm 150

Jesus,

 Remove anything from me that keeps me from rejoicing, laughing and praising when I pray. Amen.

30 INTERCEDE BY THE SPIRIT.

Likewise the Spirit also helps in our weaknesses.
For we do not know what we should pray for as we
ought, but the Spirit Himself makes intercession
for us with groanings which cannot be uttered.
—Romans 8:26

Don't know what to pray? No problem.

Don't know for whom to pray? No problem.

Don't know when to pray? No problem.

Don't know how to pray? No problem.

The Spirit knows all these things and so much more! Yield to the Spirit. Let the Holy Spirit pray through you.

When you "hit the wall" and don't know how to pray, yield to the Spirit by...

- Allowing His thoughts to be yours.
- Allowing His desires to be yours.
- Allowing His strength to be yours.
- Allowing His will to be done in you.
- Allowing His wisdom to guide you.
- Allowing His counsel to direct you.
- Allowing His comfort to encourage you.

Spirit of God,
Pray through me. Amen.

31 PRAY TO INCREASE LOVE.

And this I pray, that your love may abound still more and more in knowledge and all discernment.
—Philippians 1:9

Love intensifies as we pray. How is that? God is love. We love because He first loved us. When we commune with God in pray, we are surrounded by and indwelt richly by His love.

The more iron is in contact with electricity the more magnetized it becomes. The more we dwell in His presence, the more we abound in love. The more we pray, the more His contagious love fills and overflows us.

God's love increases the knowledge of Him. Knowledge means intimacy and closeness. Intimacy with God fosters a deeper hunger to be with Him, to pray, to worship, to adore Him more and more.

God's love intensifies discernment. Knowing spiritually what's happening...discerning spirits increases with loving God.

Pray for the love to increase so that those for whom you pray may know Him and discern the spiritual climate around them.

Jesus,
Increase the love in _____. May they know you. May they discern the spiritual climate around them rightly dividing the word of truth you give them. Amen.

32 BURY THE PAST THEN PRAY.

*They buried the bones of Saul and Jonathan his
son in the country of Benjamin in Zelah, in the
tomb of Kish his father. So they performed all that
the king commanded. And after that God heeded
the prayer for the land.*

—2 Samuel 21.14

Forget the past. Don't remember the former things (Isa.
43:18). Prayer does not change the past. But prayer can cut off
the past. Prayer confesses and repents for past sin and failure
opening the door for the Holy Spirit to set us free.

Prayer buries the past under the sea of God's forgiving
love, mercy and grace.

*He has not dealt with us according to our sins,
Nor punished us according to our iniquities.
For as the heavens are high above the earth,
So great is His mercy toward those who fear Him;
As far as the east is from the west,
So far has He removed our transgressions from us.*

—Ps. 103:9-12

The past for David was the reign of Saul and his friendship
with Jonathan. In order to be the king God called him to be,
he had to bury the past.

In order to become all Christ calls us to be, we must be a new creation with the old passing away and all things becoming new (2 Cor. 5:17).

The past reminds us of lessons learned and God's faithfulness in spite of our unfaithfulness. We can declare that God will forgive when we confess (1 Jn. 1:9).

Pray to declare God's faithfulness. Pray to cut off the past. Pray to move on with you life. Pray to get into God's new thing. Pray to die to the past and live life now to the fullest.

Jesus,

I confess and repent of the past. I declare it's cut off by the shed blood of Jesus. I step by faith into the abundant life that You have given me through your death and resurrection. Amen

33

REAP IN PRAYER WHAT YOU HAVE SOWN IN THE SPIRIT.

"Remember now, O LORD, I pray, how I have walked before You in truth and with a loyal heart, and have done what was good in Your sight." And Hezekiah wept bitterly.

—2 Kings 20:2-3

Confession isn't just a litany of past sins and failure. In Greek, the verb for "confess" means to "agree with" and "say the same as." In other words, we confess who we are from God's perspective. He sees both our strengths and our weaknesses.

Hezekiah confessed to God his strengths. God didn't need to be reminded. So why did Hezekiah bother? Was he trying to earn God's favor? Unlikely. Did he think that God had abandoned him? Possibly.

One thing was certain: *what Hezekiah had sown he would reap.* (Read Galatians 6:6-10.) What you sow in life, you can reap in prayer. Hezekiah had sown goodness, faithfulness, truthfulness and a heart full of love for God. He prayed what he had lived and he received a harvest:

Thus says the LORD, the God of David your father: "I have heard your prayer, I have seen your tears; surely I will heal you. On the third day you shall go up to the house of the LORD. And I will add to your days fifteen years. I will deliver

*you and this city from the hand of the king of
Assyria; and I will defend this city for My own
sake, and for the sake of My servant David."*
—2 Kings 20:5-6

Recall in prayer what you have sown so that you can both
break past curses and confess your coming harvest.

Lord God,
   *Bring blight and ruin to whatever I have sown
to the flesh. Bring a bountiful harvest to whatever
I have sown to the Spirit. Amen.*

34 PRAY WITH A PURE HEART.

My prayer is pure.

—Job 16:17

Jesus teaches us, "Blessed are the pure in heart, for they shall see God." (Matthew 5:8). To see the invisible requires purity in heart. To see into heaven so that you can pray what's in heaven to earth demands purity, holiness and a first-love for Jesus.

Purity speaks of moral uprightness. Stop watching, reading, or looking at immoral things. Tear down pornographic vain imaginations. "Therefore submit to God. Resist the devil and he will flee from you. Draw near to God and He will draw near to you. Cleanse your hands, you sinners; and purify your hearts, you double-minded" (James 4:7-8).

Purity speaks of being clean. Cleanse your life from dirty thoughts, actions and works. Stop telling unclean jokes. Resist listening to violent and impure things in music or on TV. Get clean. Stay clean.

Without the purity that comes from repentance and walking in the light, your prayers will be vain and ineffective. Here's the process: Confession, repentance, cleansing, walking in the light, seeing God. Pure prayer initiates the process.

Purify my heart, my walk and my life, O God.
Amen.

35 PRAY AND PRAISE DAILY.

*Prayer also will be made for Him continually,
And daily He shall be praised.*

—Psalm 72:15

"Well, I praised God yesterday."

Yesterday's praise isn't sufficient for today.

"I thanked Him last week."

Past praise grows stale like old manna.

Continual prayer and daily praise keeps us in God's presence. In an atmosphere of praise, God inhabits our relationships and guides our steps. In continual prayer God speaks to us before we talk and before we act.

If our actions and thoughts are not preceded by prayer, then they will spring from the flesh and wreck everything in their paths. If our days are not filled with praise, we will speak word curses and act selfishly.

Continual, daily prayer and praise keep us where we must dwell—in His presence. No other dwelling can give us life and hope. No other dwelling can empower us to walk in the Spirit.

God,
I praise You today! I continually confess your
Name and your Word on my lips. Amen.

36 PRAY FOR BLESSING.

Then Jacob asked, saying, "Tell me Your name, I pray." And He said, "Why is it that you ask about My name?" And He blessed him there.

—Gen. 32:29

Pray to Elohim, the God of creation. Pray to Yahweh, the "I am." Pray to El-Shaddai, the Almighty God who provides for our needs. Pray to Jehovah-Rapha, the God who heals.

Pray to El-Shammai. Be blessed by His presence. Let El-Ro'i be your shepherd. Let Adonai be your Lord.

Seeking His name brings the blessing of God's authority and power. Prayer postures receptivity. Prayer receives His power to break every curse in life.

To ask His Name is a confession that I do not have the revelation of Him that I need in my life. I can only receive that revelation by grace.

God speaks His name to that place of weakness in my life so that His strength can replace my weakness; his health can replace my sickness; his blessing can break every curse.

All I need is His Name. God's name unlocks the door to my blessing.

Too many people seek His blessing and come away empty-handed in prayer. Seek His name and His blessing will follow.

Lord,
Reveal to me Your name that will release
Your wind
    Your presence
        Your power
            Your blessing in me. Amen.

37 OBEY GOD AND RECEIVE WHAT YOU ASK.

And whatever we ask we receive from Him, because we keep His commandments and do those things that are pleasing in His sight.
—1 John 3:22

Jesus declares that when we love Him we obey Him (John 15). We live to please Him and what pleases Him is obedience, i.e. *doing those things that are pleasing in His sight.*

Disobeying? Then don't ask. When you live to please Him, you will never want to ask for anything that He doesn't want to give you.

Disobedience…

- shuts the windows of heaven.
- produces brazen heavens.
- paralyzes prayer.
- produces powerlessness

At times you may cry out, "Why isn't God answering my prayers and granting what I ask?" Now you know the possible answer—disobedience.

Before you pray…

- obey.
- please God.
- do what He commands.

Lord,

Before my every prayer, break my pride, convict my heart, show me any area of disobedience in my life. Amen.

38 Produce then ask.

You did not choose Me, but I chose you and appointed you that you should go and bear fruit, and that your fruit should remain, that whatever you ask the Father in My name He may give you.
—John 15:16, NKJV

God has already given you all that you need to produce, prosper and bear fruit. We produce little but ask for much. Yield fruit before you ask.

In prayer, come with your hands filled with offering to give to the Lord. Cain came with less than his best and displeased God. Making prayer the showcase of your lack never motivates God to give.

Prayer refuses to make lack an excuse for asking. My perspective often tells me I need more. God's perspective always expects me to produce more. I pray to produce. I produce to invest. I invest or sow in order to see a harvest in God's kingdom.

Don't pray for fruit. The fruit is your responsibility. It's the result of your sowing, tending and harvesting. Ask for the seed that you sow to bring an increase. Man plants and waters but God gives the increase.

> *God,*
>   *I bring to you an overflowing harvest, an overflowing heart an overflowing gratitude an overflowing love. Increase it, I pray. Amen.*

39 WAIT—EXPERIENCE GOD'S GOODNESS IN PRAYER.

The LORD is good to those who wait for Him, To the soul who seeks Him.

—Lamentations 3:25

Stop rushing.

Get over your stress.

Refrain from trying to push God.

Prayer waits.

Prayer welcomes the pressure.

Prayer invites God's push.

Start resting.

Be patient.

Seek of Him instead of from Him.

Waiting births expectancy.

Expectancy rejoices in hope.

Hope conquers doubt.

So wait. What's your hurry? You cannot catch the God whose has already captured your heart. Love Him patiently as you see His goodness fill your waiting.

God,
   I seek You. I wait on You. Thank you for Your goodness. Amen.

40 PRAY FROM YOUR HEART.

For You, O LORD of hosts, God of Israel, have revealed this to Your servant, saying, 'I will build you a house.' Therefore Your servant has found it in his heart to pray this prayer to You.
—Samuel 7:27

Heartfelt prayer. What is it? Praying from the heart goes beyond reason. Heartfelt prayer gets beneath the surface and reveals the deeper things in life. Heartfelt prayer is always plummeting the soul's depths and seeking what's real instead of what's religious.

Religious is a form of godliness. Religion trusts in ritual and traditions instead of relationship with God. Religion says "do." Relationship with Jesus says, "Done."

Praying from the heart confesses real not religious thoughts. Praying from the heart confesses real feelings not just hyped up emotions. Praying from the heart seeks real change instead of asking God to change others or circumstances. Pray from the heart.

Father God,
   I really think that _____

_____

_____.

Jesus,
  I really feel that _____
  _____
  _____.

Spirit of God,
  Change me so that _____
  _____
  _____.

41 PRAY SHAMELESSLY WHEN YOU'RE DESTITUTE.

He shall regard the prayer of the destitute, And shall not despise their prayer.

—Psalm 102:17

When you have nothing to bring before the Lord, pray!

When you are emotionally spent, pray!

When all your resources are depleted, pray!

When you feel weak and helpless, pray!

When depression, despair, desperation and destitution surround you, pray!

When your faith runs out and you feel like quitting, pray!

When you have no money, no work, or no way out, pray!

Destitution should drive you to do only one desperate thing—pray!

Jesus,
I'm desperate for You. Amen.

42 OBEY TO PRAY.

One who turns away his ear from hearing the law,
even his prayer is an abomination.

—Proverbs 28:9

The only way to pray when disobeying is to repent. Repentance requires not only contrition but also the conviction to stop sinning and start doing what's right.

Too often we expect God to hear and answer our prayers when we come to him with dirty hands and hearts. Clean up your act through repentance and obedience. "Therefore, having these promises, beloved, let us cleanse ourselves from all filthiness of the flesh and spirit, perfecting holiness in the fear of God" (2 Cor. 7:1).

Prayer cannot excuse or nullify the effects of disobedience. Prayer turns the heart away from disobedience to weeping contrition before God. Prayer coupled with disobedience adds insult to injury before God.

Want a powerful prayer life? **Obey God.** A key to effective prayer is your obedience. Here's the sequence of powerful pray:

Trust → Obedience → Prayer → Power

Jesus,

Teach me to trust and obey, so that when I pray, Your power will flow. Amen.

43 PRAY FOR RESTORATION.

Now when he was in affliction, he implored the LORD his God, and humbled himself greatly before the God of his fathers, He received his entreaty, heard his supplication, and brought him back to Jerusalem into his kingdom. Then Manasseh knew that the LORD was God.
—2 Chronicles 33:12-13

Not all afflictions come from the enemy or from worldly persecution. Some affliction comes upon us from the hand of the Lord (Ps. 88:7). Instead of imploring God to vindicate you when affliction comes, pray for God to reveal the source. If God has afflicted you, then…

1. Implore God. Don't run away and tried to hide. Come clean. Confess. Run to God in the midst of your affliction. Stop complaining. Don't become bitter. His affliction is to make you better not bitter.

2. Humble yourself. Let your pride be crushed. Stop protesting how victimized you have become. Refuse to assert that "I deserve better than this." Truthfully, when you have done your best, you will still fall short of His best for you. In grace, God makes up the gap between your effort and His expectation. Your best is never a reason for pride; it's only an opportunity to serve God and see God multiply what little you have done into a great harvest.

3. Entreat and supplicate. Persistently come into His presence. Prostrate yourself before Almighty God in worship and praise.

4. Receive restoration. Receiving is much different than taking. The taker believes he deserves to get what he deserves. The receiver acknowledges that he has done nothing to earn the free gift of grace coming from the Father. Receive restoration as a free gift not a right.

Are you ready to pray for restoration? Such prayer moves from self-centered to being centered on God. Restoration never happens because we deserve it; restoration always comes to the humbled supplicant who prays:

> *God,*
> *Restore me to Your presence, so that I may worship and serve You—receiving your restoration so that I may continually be in Your presence. Amen.*

44 PRAY BECAUSE GOD IS FAITHFUL.

Hear my prayer, O LORD, Give ear to my supplications! In Your faithfulness answer me, and in Your righteousness.

—Psalm 143:1

If prayer depended on our faithfulness, then nothing would ever be accomplished by prayer. Often…

- We forget to pray.
- We are too tired to pray.
- We lack the conviction and commitment to follow through on what we have prayed.

Pray works not because we are faithful but because He is faithful. In His faithfulness, our prayers get answered. Because of His righteousness, our prayers enter into the Holy of Holies.

When you are unfaithful, the enemy will tempt you with these thoughts:

- You have failed in prayer so God will abandon you.
- You lack strength so you're too weak to arouse God's attention.
- You vacillate too much; no sense in trying to focus or center on God.

But our loving Father says to you:

- I'm always available even when you're not.
- I'm always strong even when you're not.
- I'm always focused on you even when you can't focus on me.

So, what to do? Pray. Prayerlessness allows the enemy to rob you of the very thing God wants to give you. Only come to the Father and ask.

> *Lord,*
> *I thank you for your faithfulness. How I need You. Your strength. Your righteousness. Your availability. Thank You, Lord, for always being there for me. Amen.*

45 PRAY FOR JERUSALEM'S PEACE.

Pray for the peace of Jerusalem: "May they prosper who love you."

—Psalm 122:6

The peace of Jerusalem may seem hopeless but consider this: *Jerusalem will know peace when the Prince of Peace reigns there.*

With the peace of Jerusalem comes the Messiah's reign.

With the peace of Jerusalem comes healing and health.

With the peace of Jerusalem comes the cessation of war.

With the peace of Jerusalem comes the Kingdom of God. (Read Isaiah 11)

O God,
I pray for the peace of Jerusalem... For that day when the lion will lie down with the lamb, for that day when swords will be beaten into plowshares, for that day when the law of love will be written on every person's heart, for that day when the Prince of Peace will sit upon His throne in Jerusalem. Amen.

46 Pray in His house.

Even them I will bring to My holy mountain, And make them joyful in My house of prayer. Their burnt offerings and their sacrifices will be accepted on My altar; For My house shall be called a house of prayer for all nations."
— Isaiah 56:7

How precious little time is really spent in prayer in His House!

You are His house. Within a day's rush and bustle, how much time and effort is devoted within you to prayer? Compare your time in prayer with your time eating, driving, working or playing.

The Church is His house. Much time is spent singing, preaching and making announcement. Time is expended in offering, greeting, communion and fellowship. But what about prayer? What percentage of any worship service is actually devoted to prayer?

What distinctive does His house have? Dancing? Contemporary worship? Praise? Awesome messages? Loving fellowship? Moving music? All of these may be present but only prayer invites His presence.

Let it be said of us—we prayed. Let it be said of our churches—they prayed.

Lord,
   Make of us houses of prayer. Amen.

47 CONFESS HIS RIGHTEOUSNESS NOT YOURS.

"O Lord, according to all Your righteousness, I pray, let Your anger and Your fury be turned away from Your city Jerusalem, Your holy mountain; because for our sins, and for the iniquities of our fathers, Jerusalem and Your people are a reproach to all those around us."

—Daniel 9:16

We have come to believe that our righteousness can make demands upon God in prayer. The more good works we do, the more we expect God to reward us. The more we give; the more we expect to get. The more we confess His ways, the more we expect to get our way.

The road into His presence has been paved by Jesus' broken body and shed blood. Daniel confessed the sins of his people pleading for the righteousness of God to turn away wrath.

For the sake of a few righteous people in Sodom, Abraham bargained with God to spare the city. For the sake of one righteousness man, Jesus, we can trust God to save, heal and deliver.

Lord Jesus,
We come before You with guilty lives asking You to spare us not because we are righteous, but for the sake of Your righteousness. Amen.

48 STAY THE WATCH.

"Watch and pray, lest you enter into temptation.
The spirit indeed is willing, but the flesh is weak."
—Matthew 26:41

Stay the watch. Don't retire before your watch is over and you've been relieved. Be alert. It's never too late and you're never too tired to pray.

When the flesh is weak, don't try to stay the watch alone. Get help and support.

- Pray with a prayer partner.
- Ask the Spirit to help you pray.
- Pray the Word of God.
- Pray in the Spirit.
- Gather with other saints to worship and prayer.
- Pray in different positions of prayer—standing, kneeling, lying prostrate, walking, lifting holy hands and bowing in prayer.
- Fast and prayer.
- Worship, sing, praise and shout your prayer.

Scripture commands us to rest. Pray when you're rested. Take care of the temple of your body. Watching and praying gives you the strength to resist temptation.

God,
Empower me to stay the watch. Amen.

49 BELIEVE WHEN ASKING.

Therefore I say to you, whatever things you ask when you pray, believe that you receive them, and you will have them.

—Mark 11:24

How can we pray with confidence? First, we pray His will not ours be done. If what we pray is His will, then we can be confident that God will grant us our request.

Second, we pray with a pure heart to see God. We see ourselves and our situations from His perspective and not our own. We seek God's timing, purpose and glory when we pray. Pray is always about God. We come before God never to demand what we want. We seek what He wants.

Finally, we pray with faith. In other words, our trust is in God not in our prayers. Some people have faith in faith. You can believe with all the passion you wish and still not see an answer. But you can pray passionately loving God and see His answer every time.

Jesus,
Help me to fix my eyes on You in prayer.
Deepen my trust in You. Show me Your will so that
I may always pray, Your will not mine be done.
Amen.

50 WITHDRAW TO THE WILDERNESS TO PRAY.

*So He Himself often withdrew into the wilderness
and prayed.*

—Luke 5:16

What is it that makes the wilderness so conducive to prayer?

The wilderness increases our thirst for living water. The dryer our lives become, the greater we thirst for the living water that only Jesus can give. Jesus promised, "Whoever drinks of the water that I shall give him will never thirst. But the water that I shall give him will become in him a fountain of water springing up into everlasting life" (John 4:14).

The wilderness lays bare the reality that life is a lonely journey. Few friends welcome entering the wilderness with you. Fewer still can withstand the temptations that arise in the wilderness. Alone Jesus faced temptation in the wilderness.

The wilderness brings you closer to God. You never enter the wilderness alone. Jesus is with you always. While the wilderness exposes just how lonely life is, it also reveals just how close God is.

Withdraw with me, Lord Jesus, into the wilderness. There, feed me the bread of life. There, satisfy my thirst with Your living water. There draw close to me. Amen.

51 PRAY FOR HARVEST WORKERS.

Then He said to them, "The harvest truly is great,
but the laborers are few; therefore pray the Lord of
the harvest to send out laborers into His harvest.
　　　　　　　　　　　　　　　　　—Luke 10:2

Often people admonish one another to pray for souls. Surprisingly, Jesus instructs us to pray for workers. The fact is that the souls are ready. So many are hungry for the gospel but so few are willing to make the personal sacrifice to go into the harvest. Still fewer pray for those workers to go.

Why is that? We are too satisfied with minimal results. A few saved souls really excite us. Of course, every saved soul is precious to God but why not go after the whole harvest instead of just a few?

Remember: harvesting is expensive. It's relatively inexpensive to sow. It's more expensive to tend the fields. But the greatest expense is in the harvest. Are you willing to pay the price and count the cost of the harvest? The first expense is this: *prayer.*

Prayer fills the heart of the workers with a compassion for the lost. Prayer presses the workers into an urgency to reach the lost. Prayer opens the eyes of the workers to the plight of the lost. Prayer excites the workers with the abundance of the harvest. So pray for harvest workers!

Jesus,
　　Send workers into the harvest. Send me. Amen.

52 Don't lose heart; always pray.

Then He spoke a parable to them, that men always ought to pray and not lose heart.

—Luke 18:1

What tempts us to lose heart?

When the answers seem to take so long in coming.

When we are tired.

When other persecute us for praying.

When we let stress and busyness control us.

When others will not pray with us.

When love waxes cold.

When faith melts under the heat of doubt.

What helps us take heart to pray?

When we pray with others.

When we wait and watch.

When we guard our hearts and mind with Christ.

When our bones wax hot with the Word.

When our eyes see miracles and faith builds.

When we pray in spite of how we feel.

Jesus,

Transplant a new heart into my life. Give me the heart to pray! Amen.

53 PRAY FOR MERCY.

God, be merciful to me a sinner!

—Luke 18:13

In prayer all pretense melts away leaving us to face the stark reality of who we are not who we would like to be.

In prayer our greatest needs are exposed along with our greatest sins.

In prayer, we cry out for mercy because nothing else can be uttered.

In prayer, we desperately seek for us what we cannot do for ourselves—forgiveness.

In prayer, we don't care who listens or what they think of us. All that matters is what God thinks of us.

In prayer, God's mercy reminds me of my complete inability to forgive myself much less others.

In prayer, I confess that until I receive mercy, I have nothing else to pray.

Praying this mercy prayer offends the self-righteous. Not praying it leaves me mired in offense.

Lord,
Be merciful to me, a sinner. Amen.

54 CELEBRATE BEING PRAYED FOR.

I [Jesus] pray for them. I do not pray for the world but for those whom You have given Me, for they are Yours.

—John 17:9

The Lord's prayer traditionally ascribed to the prayer in Matthew 6 was actually "The Disciples' Prayer" that they, and we, are to pray to the Father. So, the real "Lord's Prayer" that Jesus prayed for us is in John 17.

We are to pray as He prayed—for one another. We pray that saints will not fall into temptation. We pray that saints will live pure and holy lives. We pray that saints prosper and be in good health.

Praying for one another keeps us in touch with needs, concerns and miracles. When God answers the prayer for another, we can really get excited. We are witnesses to a miracle.

Rejoice and celebrate that Jesus continues to pray for you eternally before the throne of God. Celebrate and dance for joy that His intercession is always effective.

Follow His example. Pray for the saints.

List the saints whom you will pray for today:

_____

_____

_____

55 DON'T WORRY ABOUT ANYTHING; PRAY!

Be anxious for nothing, but in everything by prayer and supplication, with thanksgiving, let your requests be made known to God.
—Philippians 4:6

Do you spend more time worrying than praying? Has anxiety hindered your prayer life? Jesus instructs us, "But seek first the kingdom of God and His righteousness, and all these things shall be added to you. Therefore do not worry about tomorrow, for tomorrow will worry about its own things. Sufficient for the day is its own trouble" (Matt. 6:33).

Worry wastes time; prayer sows into eternity.

Worry focuses on self; prayer focuses on God.

Worry fosters doubt; prayer builds faith.

Worry squanders hope; prayer embraces hope.

Worry declares things impossible; prayer knows that nothing is impossible with God.

Worry dreads tomorrow; prayer knows the best is yet to come.

With worry nothing is accomplished; with prayer the work of God's kingdom goes forward.

Jesus,
I give You my worry! Amen.

56 PRAY FOR DELIVERANCE.

For I know that this will turn out for my deliverance through Your prayer and the supply of the Spirit of Jesus Christ.

—Philippians 1:19

The gospel declares that Jesus saves, heals and delivers us. Jesus saves us from sin and for eternal life with Him. Jesus heals us physically and emotionally. Jesus delivers us from the bondages of past sin, curses, strongholds, diseases and failures.

When others are bound by addictions, abuse, abandonment and afflictions, apply the prescription that God provides—prayer. Go to the Great Physician and ask Him to deliver them.

No ritual or formula is needed. Jesus provided us with the example. He simply spoke the word of deliverance and people were set free. Pray like this: "Come out of them, in Jesus' name."

People are delivered by prayer and the supply of the Spirit of Jesus Christ. Through prayer become the instrument of the Spirit's delivering power in the lives of others.

> *Spirit of God,*
> *Pray through me to deliver others, breaking every yoke of bondage and declaring the liberty of Christ Jesus. Amen.*

57 INTERCEDE WITH CHRIST IN THE SECRET PLACE.

Who is he who condemns? It is Christ who died, and furthermore is also risen, who is even at the right hand of God, who also makes intercession for us.

—Romans 8:34

Where is the secret place of prayer? It's not a physical place even though you may have your favorite retreat or closet of prayer.

Jesus instructs, "But you, when you pray, go into your room, and when you have shut your door, pray to your Father who is in the **secret place;** and your Father who sees in secret will reward you openly" (Matt. 6:6).

That secret place of prayer is in the **heavenly places**: "and raised us up together, and made us sit together in the heavenly places in Christ Jesus" (Eph. 2:6).

That secret place of prayer is in the **shadow of the Almighty:** "He who dwells in the secret place of the Most High shall abide under the shadow of the Almighty" (Ps. 91:1).

In that secret place of prayer, we can hide in the **presence of God:** "You shall hide them in the secret place of Your presence" (Ps. 31:20).

No matter how weak we feel or shaken or lives may become as we reel under pressures and stress, in the secret place **we stand on the Rock:**

In the secret place of His tabernacle
He shall hide me;
He shall set me high upon a rock.

—Psalm 27:5

In that secret place, **we pray with Christ** as He intercedes for us. We pray His will for us. We listen to His words and heart and pray what He prays.

For no earthly reason we may find ourselves praying for a city, a nation, a person or a situation unknown to you in the natural. How does that happen? God has raised us into the heavenly places. There we hear the prayer of Jesus. By His Spirit, we enter into the secret place of prayer.

The prayer of the secret place releases miracles we may never know of until we step into eternal life.

The prayer of the secret place provides provision for which others are desperate.

The prayer of the secret place releases healing into the sick lives of those we have never met.

The prayer of the secret place moves beyond what we know into the revelation of what He knows. It is often the inexpressible prayer of travail and moaning given to us by the Spirit.

The prayer of the secret place moves us from praying to Christ into praying with Christ. It takes us from doing our work into doing His work: "Most assuredly, I say to you, he who believes in Me, the works that I do he will do also; and greater works than these he will do, because I go to My Father. And whatever you ask in My name, that I will do, that the Father may be glorified in the Son. 14 If you ask anything in My name, I will do it" (John 14:12-14).

Father,
   Hide me in your secret place.

Jesus,
   Let me hear your intercession that I may know how to pray.

Holy Spirit,
   Intercede through me to accomplish Your eternal will. Amen.

58 Confess your sin and the sins of others.

Now while I was speaking, praying, and confessing my sin and the sin of my people Israel, and presenting my supplication before the LORD my God for the holy mountain of my God.
—Daniel 9:20

Isn't it enough that I confess my own sins? Why is it that I must also confess the sins of others?

Because in prayer we stand in the gap for others. Not only do our personal sins bind us; the corporate sins of our family, community, church and nation hinder us.

When you confess sin, begin with your own personal transgressions, but don't stop there. Be cleansed of the corporate sins of those around you. Personal confession frees you to move around in your own territory, but what a small arena of power and influence that may be.

Corporate confession frees you to move into realms of intercession far beyond your personal sphere of influence. It moves you into warring against principalities and powers:

"Finally, my brethren, be strong in the Lord and in the power of His might. Put on the whole armor of God, that you may be able to stand against the wiles of the devil. For we do not wrestle against flesh and blood, but against principalities, against powers, against the rulers of the darkness of this age, against spiritual hosts of wickedness in the heavenly places" (Eph. 6:10-12).

Almighty God,

I confess my sins and the sins of my family, my church, my community, my nation.

I stand firm against the principalities and powers that would seek to bind us up and render us powerless.

I boldly put on the armor of God, standing firm against the evil one, praying for all the saints, declaring victory over every evil in Jesus' name. Amen.

59 PRAY FOR WISDOM.

If any of you lacks wisdom, let him ask of God, who gives to all liberally and without reproach, and it will be given to him.

—James 1:5

Wisdom sees everything from God's perspective. My perspective can only see what's visible and what's locked in time and space. But from God's perspective I can see myself and others as He sees us. From God's perspective I can take the long look into what's best for both now and the future.

Wisdom lines up knowledge and understanding so that I may walk a straight path in God's ways.

Knowledge is the revelation of His truth through His Word that keeps us from sin and directs us in the paths of righteousness for His name's sake. Knowledge brings me into an intimacy with Him so that I may hear his voice before I take the next step in my spiritual walk.

Understanding applies correctly what God has revealed to me. With understanding I can do the new thing that God has shown me without fear of failure.

God's Word declares, "For the LORD gives wisdom; From His mouth come knowledge and understanding" (Prov. 2:6). Want God's perspective? Pray for wisdom.

Lord God,

Give me wisdom that I may see what You see. Give me knowledge that I may know You. Give me understanding that I may do Your will. Amen.

60 PRAY THE WORD.

*Remember, I pray, the word that You commanded
Your servant Moses.*

—Nehemiah 1:8

Praying God's Word doesn't remind God of what He needs to do. Praying God's Word reminds us of His promises so that we might release the power of His Word into this hour for His will and glory to be revealed.

In the following pages of action-truths, I am encouraging you to pray the Word. Space is provided for you to pray insert your name and/or the names of others.

I am not commenting on the scriptures. Simply pray them. Take time to pray out loud. Pray for everyone that God places on your heart.

Praying God's Word speaks that promise or truth of God into this moment of time and space.

Praying God's Word births promise into the *now* of our lives. Praying God's Word declares His will for us. Praying God's Word takes prayer from the realm of my thoughts into His thoughts.

Pray the word! Begin by praying Psalm 119:10-16:

> *With my whole heart I have sought You;*
> *Oh, let me not wander from Your commandments!*
> *Your word I have hidden in my heart,*

That I might not sin against You!
Blessed are You, O LORD!
Teach me Your statutes!
With my lips I have declared
All the judgments of Your mouth.
I have rejoiced in the way of Your testimonies,
As much as in all riches.
I will meditate on Your precepts,
And contemplate Your ways.
I will delight myself in Your statutes;
I will not forget Your word. Amen.

61 PRAY BLESSING.

The LORD bless _____ and keep _____;
the LORD make His face shine upon _____,
And be gracious to _____;
the LORD lift up His countenance upon _____,
and give _____ peace.

(based on Numbers 6:24-26)

62 PRAY NURTURE.

The LORD is _____'s shepherd; _____ shall
* not want.*
He makes _____ to lie down in green pastures;
He leads _____ beside the still waters.
He restores _____'s soul;
He leads _____ in the paths of righteousness for
* His name's sake.*
Yea, though _____ walk through the valley of
* the shadow of death, _____ will fear no evil;*
For You are with _____;
Your rod and Your staff, they comfort_____.
You prepare a table before _____ in the presence
* of _____'s enemies;*
You anoint _____'s head with oil;
_____'s cup runs over.
Surely goodness and mercy shall follow _____ all
* the days of _____'s life;*
And _____ will dwell in the house of the LORD
* forever. Amen.*

(based on Psalm 23)

63 CONFESS YOUR SINS.

Have mercy upon _____, O God,

According to Your lovingkindness;

According to the multitude of Your tender mercies,

Blot out _____'s transgressions.

Wash _____ thoroughly from _____'s iniquity,

And cleanse me from _____'s sin.

For I acknowledge _____'s transgressions,

And _____'s sin is always before _____.

Against You, You only, has _____ sinned,

And done this evil in Your sight—

That You may be found just when You speak,

And blameless when You judge. Amen.

(based on Ps. 51:1-4)

64 Pray protection.

_____ who dwells in the secret place of the Most
   High
Shall abide under the shadow of the Almighty.
_____ *will say of the LORD, "He is my refuge
   and my fortress;*
My God, in Him _____ *will trust."*
Surely He shall deliver _____
from the snare of the fowler
And from the perilous pestilence.
He shall cover _____ *with His feathers,*
And under His wings _____ *shall take refuge;*
His truth shall be _____ *'s shield and buckler.*
_____ *shall not be afraid of the terror by night,*
Nor of the arrow that flies by day,
Nor of the pestilence that walks in darkness,
Nor of the destruction that lays waste at noonday.
   Amen.

(based on Psalm 91:1-6)

65 PRAY TO GUARD YOUR HEART.

I pray that _____ will give attention to God's
  words;

Let _____ incline his/her ear to God's sayings.

Do not let them depart from _____'s eyes;

Keep them in the midst of _____'s heart;

For they are life to_____,

And health to _____'s flesh.

Lord, keep _____'s heart with all diligence,

For out of it spring the issues of life.

Put away from _____ a deceitful mouth,

And put perverse lips far from _____.

Let _____'s eyes look straight ahead,

And _____'s eyelids look right before you.

Help _____ ponder the path of _____'s feet,

And let all of _____'s ways be established. Amen.

(based on Proverbs 4:19-26)

66 Pray praise.

Bless the LORD, O _____'s soul;

And all that is within _____, bless His holy
  name!

Bless the LORD, O _____'s soul,

And forget not all His benefits:

Who forgives all _____'s iniquities,

Who heals all _____'s diseases,

Who redeems _____'s life from destruction,

Who crowns _____ with lovingkindness and
  tender mercies,

Who satisfies _____'s mouth with good things,

So that _____'s youth is renewed like the eagle's.

(based on Psalm 103:1-5)

67 Pray prosperity.

Blessed is _____

Who walks not in the counsel of the ungodly,

Nor stands in the path of sinners,

Nor sits in the seat of the scornful;

But _____ *'s delight is in the law of the LORD,*

And in His law _____ *meditates day and night.*

_____ *shall be like a tree*

Planted by the rivers of water,

That brings forth its fruit in its season,

Whose leaf also shall not wither;

And whatever _____ *does shall prosper.*

(based on Psalm 1:1-3)

68 PRAY HEALING.

Surely He has borne _____'s griefs

And carried _____'s sorrows;

Yet _____ esteemed Him stricken,

Smitten by God, and afflicted.

But He was wounded for _____'s transgressions,

He was bruised for _____'s iniquities;

The chastisement for _____'s peace was upon
*   Him,*

And by His stripes _____ is healed.

(based on Isaiah 53:3-5)

69 PRAY LOVE FOR YOUR MATE.

_____ *is patient,*

_____ *is kind.*

_____ *does not envy,*

_____ *does not boast,*

_____ *is not proud.*

_____ *is not rude,*

_____ *is not self-seeking,*

_____ *is not easily angered,*

_____ *keeps no record of wrongs.*

_____ *does not delight in evil but rejoices with*
the truth.

_____ *always protects, always trusts, always*
hopes, always perseveres.

(based on 1 Cor. 13:3-8 NIV)

70 PRAY VICTORY.

In Christ Jesus, in all things _____ is more than a conqueror through Him who loved us. For _____ is persuaded that neither death nor life, nor angels nor principalities nor powers, nor things present nor things to come, nor height nor depth, nor any other created thing, shall be able to separate _____ from the love of God which is in Christ Jesus our Lord. Amen.

(based on Romans 8:37-39)

71 PRAY INHERITANCE.

*In Him _____ has redemption through Jesus'
blood, the forgiveness of sins, according to the riches
of His grace which He made to abound toward
_____ in all wisdom and prudence, having made
known to _____ the mystery of His will,
according to His good pleasure which He purposed
in Himself, that in the dispensation of the fullness
of the times He might gather together in one all
things in Christ, both which are in heaven and
which are on earth—in Him.*

*In Christ also _____ has obtained an
inheritance, being predestined according to the
purpose of Him who works all things according to
the counsel of His will, that _____ who first
trusted in Christ should be to the praise of His
glory.*

(based on Ephesians 1:7-13)

72 PRAY TO BE INDWELT BY CHRIST.

For this reason I bow my knees to the Father of our Lord Jesus Christ, from whom the whole family in heaven and earth is named, that He would grant _____, according to the riches of His glory, to be strengthened with might through His Spirit in the inner man, that Christ may dwell in _____'s heart through faith; that _____, being rooted and grounded in love, may be able to comprehend with all the saints what is the width and length and depth and height— to know the love of Christ which passes knowledge; that _____ may be filled with all the fullness of God.

Now to Him who is able to do exceedingly abundantly above all that _____ asks or thinks, according to the power that works in _____, to Him be glory in the church by Christ Jesus to all generations, forever and ever. Amen.

(based on Ephesians 3:14-4:1)

73 PRAY TO SHATTER ANXIETY.

Lord Jesus, I pray that _____ will rejoice in the Lord always. Again _____ will say, rejoice! Let _____'s gentleness be known to all men. My _____ be anxious for nothing, but in everything by prayer and supplication, with thanksgiving, let _____'s requests be made known to God; and the peace of God, which surpasses all understanding, will guard _____'s heart and mind through Christ Jesus. Amen.

(based on Philippians 4:4-7)

74 PRAY FOR ANOINTING.

Father,

May the Spirit of the Lord GOD be upon _____,

Because the LORD has anointed _____

To preach good tidings to the poor;

He has sent _____ to heal the brokenhearted,

To proclaim liberty to the captives,

And the opening of the prison to those who are bound;

To proclaim the acceptable year of the LORD,

And the day of vengeance of our God;

To comfort all who mourn,

To console those who mourn in Zion,

To give them beauty for ashes,

The oil of joy for mourning,

The garment of praise for the spirit of heaviness;

That they may be called trees of righteousness,

The planting of the LORD, that He may be glorified. Amen.

(based on Isaiah 61:1-4)

75 PRAY FOR THE FAMILY.

God,

Let _____ and _____'s family hear: The LORD their God, the LORD is one! They shall love the LORD your God with all their heart, with all their soul, and with all their strength.

I pray that _____'s family will obey the commands of God and that those commands will be in their hearts. I pray that _____ shall teach them diligently to their children, and shall talk of them when they sit in _____'s house, when they walk by the way, when they lie down, and when they rise up.

May they bind them as a sign on their hand, and they shall be as frontlets between their eyes. May they write them on the doorposts of their house and on their gates. Amen.

(based on Deuteronomy 6:4-9)

76 PRAY FOR PURPOSE AND POWER.

I ask you, Lord Jesus, to do whatever Your hand and Your purpose determined before to be done.

Now, Lord, look on the threats of others, and grant to _____ that with all boldness _____ may speak Your word, by stretching out Your hand to heal, and that signs and wonders may be done by _____ through the name of Your holy Servant Jesus. Amen.

(based on Acts 4:28-30)

77 PRAY FOR JESUS TO RETURN.

Lord Jesus,

You are the Root and the Offspring of David,
the Bright and Morning Star. Even so, come, Lord
Jesus! Maranatha! Amen.

(based on Revelation 22:16-20)

OTHER BOOKS BY DR. LARRY KEEFAUVER

Inviting God's Presence

Lord, I Wish My Husband Would Pray with Me

Lord, I Wish My Teenager Would Talk with Me

Lord, I Wish My Family Would Get Saved

Hugs for Grandparents

Hugs for Heroes

When God Doesn't Heal Now

Experiencing the Holy Spirit

Praying with Smith Wigglesworth

Smith Wigglesworth on Prayer

Smith Wigglesworth on Faith

Smith Wigglesworth on Healing

Healing Words

The 77 Irrefutable Truths of Parenting

The 77 Irrefutable Truths of Marriage

The 77 Irrefutable Truths of Prayer

I'm Praying for You, Friend

I'm Praying for You, Mom

The Holy Spirit Encounter Guides (Anointing, Welcoming the Spirit, Gifts, Power, The Spirit-Led Life, River, Fire)

Commanding Angels

CONFERENCES AND SEMINARS

Growing Spiritually in Marriage
Proactive Parenting Seminars
77 Irrefutable Truths of Ministry
A Holy Spirit Encounter
The Presence-Driven Life, Family and Church
Inviting God's Presence
Prayer That Works!

FOR INFORMATION OR TO ORDER BOOKS CONTACT:

Dr. Larry Keefauver
Your Ministry Counseling Services
P.O. Box 950596
Lake Mary, Fl 32795
800-750-5306 (Voice) 407-324-5006 (fax)
Email: lkeefauv@bellsouth.net
   or larry@ymcs.org
Website: www.ymcs.org

If you were encouraged by *77 Irrefutable Truths of Prayer,* you will want to read the Keefauvers' previous book in the series, *77 Irrefutable Turths of Marriage*.

Dr. Larry & Judi Keefauver

Seventy Seven
Irrefutable Truths
of Marriage